the treasury of

Clean
Church

Jokes

W9-AVS-231

Tal D. Bonham

BROADMAN
&HOLMAN
PUBLISHERS

Nashville, Tennessee

Look for the other books in
The Treasury of Clean Jokes series:

Clean
Church
Jokes

4263-63
0-8054-6363-1

Published by Broadman & Holman Publishers,
Nashville, Tennessee
Acquisitions and Development Editor: Janis Whipple
Page Design: Desktop Miracles, Inc., Addison, Texas

Dewey Decimal Classification: 808.87
Subject Heading: JOKES
Library of Congress Card Catalog Number: 96-29826

**Library of Congress
Cataloging-in-Publication Data**
Bonham, Tal D., 1934–91.
　　The treasury of clean church jokes /
　　Tal D. Bonham. — 2nd. ed.
　　　　p.　cm.
　　　ISBN 0-8054-6363-1 (pbk.)
　　　1. Church—Humor.　I. Title.
　　PN6231.C35B66　　1997
　　818'.54020803823—dc21

96-29826
CIP

97 98 99 00 01 1 2 3 4 5

Dedication

In 1991, Tal Bonham passed away,
leaving a legacy of both love and humor
to his family and friends,
and a legacy of laughter to all his readers.
In revising
The Treasury of Clean Church Jokes,
the publisher asked his wife
for a new dedication written
in memory of Tal D. Bonham.

In the past five years, since my husband's
heavenly homecoming,
his humor has enabled me,
my family, and those who loved him
to cope with his loss.
Our four children agreed, at the time of
selecting the Scripture inscription
on his tombstone, that the
following would be appropriate—

"A merry heart doeth good like a medicine"
(Prov. 17:22).
—Faye Bonham

Dedication

Generally—To the unsung hero around the church office—the secretary

Specifically—To the secretaries who did the work for which I received credit—Ethel, Darlis, Trudy, Minnie, Carolyn, and Opal

More Specifically—To the secretaries at the Baptist Building on Broad in Columbus, Ohio

And Even More Specifically—To Esther Lafferty, my present secretary

Acknowledgments

I give a special word of appreciation and love to those churches which have allowed me to be their pastor. Thank you, Lightning Ridge Baptist Church near Ada, Oklahoma, where I served during college days. Thank you, Caney Baptist Church in Caney, Oklahoma; and Midway Baptist Church in Pernell, Oklahoma, where I served during seminary days. Thank you, First Baptist Church in Marlow, Oklahoma; and South Side Baptist Church in Pine Bluff, Arkansas. All allowed me to be your pastor and to enjoy it. We both laughed and cried together through the years.

This book could not have been completed without the help of Robert Larremore and Mr. and Mrs. Charles Tommey. Thanks, dear friends, for helping to put it all together.

And, to Faye, my wife of almost three decades—you truly light up my life and help me to see the best and funniest in the lives of others.

Contents

Introduction

The funniest things happen at church. Have you listened lately?

One young pastor preached a lengthy sermon on Samson and inadvertently referred to him as "Tarzan."

A music director announced, "Now let us turn over in our hymnals to page 43!" Did you ever try to "turn over" in a hymn book?

A pastor pleaded, "Now let us have a word of prayer for those who are sick in the bulletin." How sick is one who is *in the bulletin?*

One pastor at prayer meeting asked all who had special prayer requests to raise their hands. His mind must have been on a recently stormy business meeting at the church as he replied, "All those opposed by the same sign."

An evangelist begged passionately for someone to make a decision during the invitation. Finally, after several verses of the invitation hymn, a young lad started forward. The evangelist exclaimed, "And a little child shall lead them!" The boy walked all the way to the front of the church toward the pastor, made a right turn, and walked out into the hall en route to the bathroom!

A pastor recalled the Sunday morning service when two women came to the service together. One, recently widowed, became upset during the service and left. Her friend, obviously wanting to help, got up to leave, stepped into the aisle, and fell down. She climbed up, started again, and fell again. She got up, started the third time, and fell again! The compassionate pastor called the home of the stumbling church member soon after the service to inquire about her difficulty. Her laughing husband answered the phone and said, "Her foot went to sleep!" The pastor retorted, "I accept no responsibility for putting people's feet to sleep!"

Some might wonder if it is proper to laugh at church. To answer that question you need to answer another question: Does God have a sense of humor? Certainly! As one Christian comedian put it, "I know God has a sense of humor because He created me!"

Certainly Jesus enjoyed humor. In fact, many Bible scholars are discovering that Jesus made extensive use of humor in his preaching and teaching. It would not have been uncommon at all for those who heard Him to laugh. After all, if you couldn't laugh around Jesus, where could you laugh?

Now, here comes a book of clean church jokes. Clean? Yes, hopefully, with no trace of sacrilege or crudeness often used by those who share religious humor.

Through the years, I heard some of these jokes at conventions, crusades, church services, and conferences. I hope you enjoy them as much as I have enjoyed collecting them.

Hold this page to your face and blow on it. If it turns:

Green—call your physician.

Brown—see your dentist.

Purple—consult your psychiatrist.

Red—see your banker.

Yellow—call your lawyer to make a will.

If it remains the same color, you're in good health, and there is no reason on earth why you should not be in church this week.

Adam and Eve

History has recorded only one indispensable man: Adam.

After the fall in the garden of Eden, Adam was walking with his sons, Cain and Abel. They passed by the ruins of the garden of Eden. One of the boys asked, "What's that?"

Adam replied, "Boys, that's where your mother ate us out of house and home."

What a good thing Adam had going. When he said something, he knew nobody had said it before.

Sunday School teacher: "What evidence is there in the Bible that Adam and Eve were noisy?"
Boy: "They raised Cain!"

Sunday School teacher: "Can anyone tell me the story of Adam and Eve?"
Abbie: "First, God created Adam. Then He looked at him and said, 'I think I could do better if I tried again.' So He created Eve."

Did Adam and Eve Argue?
About What?
"You've put my shirt in the salad again, Eve!"

Adam and Eve were the first bookkeepers. They invented the looseleaf system.

Question: Why didn't Adam and Eve use calculators and computers?
Answer: Because the Lord told them to multiply on the face of the earth.

The story of Adam and Eve was being carefully explained in the children's Sunday School class. Following the story, the children were asked to draw a picture that would illustrate the story.

Little Fred was most interested and drew a picture of a car with three people in it. In the front seat behind the wheel was a man and in the back seat, a man and woman.

The teacher was at a loss to understand how this illustrated the lesson of Adam and Eve.

But little Johnny was prompt with his explanation: "Why, this is God driving Adam and Eve out of the garden!"

A little boy was asked to name the first man. He promptly answered, "Adam."

Then, he was asked to name the first woman. He pondered long and hard and finally suggested, "Madam."

Announcements

A minister was opening his mail one morning. Drawing a single sheet of paper from an envelope, he found written on it only one word: "Fool."

The next Sunday he announced, "I have known many people who have written letters and forgot to sign their names. But this week I received a letter from someone who signed his name but forgot to write the letter."

A pastor had a practice of leaving his pulpit for a brief time during the morning service. While one of his staff made the announcements, he went to tell a Bible story to the children in children's church.

One new member didn't understand. One day he said to the minister, "Pastor, you're the first preacher I ever saw who takes a coffee break during the service."

Pastor's Announcement before Offering: "I would like to remind you that what you are about to give is deductible, cannot be taken with you, and is considered in the Bible to be the root of all evil."

"There will be a meeting of the Board immediately after the service," announced the pastor. After the close of the service, the group gathered at the back of the auditorium for the announced meeting. Yet there was a stranger in their midst. He was a visitor who had never attended their church before.

"My friend," asked the pastor, "did you understand that this is a meeting of the Board?"

"Yes," said the visitor, "and after that sermon, I'm about as *bored* as you can get!"

A preacher phoned the city's newspaper. "Thank you very much," said he, "for the error you made when you announced my sermon topic for last Sunday. The topic I sent you was 'What Jesus Saw in a Publican.' You printed it as 'What Jesus Saw in a Republican.' I had the biggest crowd of the year!"

Announcement on bulletin board: "Why is it that there is never enough time to do things right, but there is always enough time to do things over?"

The chairman of the pastor search committee informed the congregation: "Next Sunday our visiting preacher will be the Rev. Joe Doaks. If you would like to see the other preachers, you will find them hanging in the vestibule."

Baptism

The country church was located so far out in the woods that there was no indoor plumbing. However, since baptism was such an important part of the church's life, they improvised by building a baptistry under the pulpit. When it came time to baptize, they would move the pulpit to the side, open the trap door, fill the baptistry with water hauled in by a large tank truck, drop some wooden stairs down into it, and string up some curtains.

The thick curtains were carefully hung on wires. One curtain served as a backdrop to the baptistry as it was pulled around in a circular position. The curtains were also arranged in such a way as to provide a men's dressing room on one side of the baptistry and a women's dressing room on the other side of the baptistry.

The young pastor of this country church was to baptize his first two candidates—an elderly man and a very heavyset lady.

"Shouldn't we offer to help our young pastor?" asked one of the deacons. It was decided that the deacons would give special attention to the elderly man lest he fall on the slick wooden steps.

On the evening of the baptismal service, one deacon waited in the baptistry with the pastor, and another deacon carefully helped the elderly gentleman down the stairs. After he was baptized, the deacon in the baptistry helped him up the stairs and followed him back behind the curtains to the dressing room.

No one, however, thought to help the young pastor with the baptism of the heavyset lady. Excitedly, she stepped into the baptistry on the first step. The wooden steps, slick from standing under water so long, proved to be her downfall. Her feet slipped, and she promptly sat down on the top step. Then, one by one, she bounced down into the baptistry in the sitting position.

They claim you could hear her scream a mile away. Screaming and bouncing down the stairs, she reached up to grab the only object available—the curtains! So, down into the baptistry with the screaming lady came the men's dressing room and the women's dressing room!

There, visible to the eyes of the whole congregation on one side of the baptistry was the elderly gentleman in the process of getting dressed. He had already donned his longhandled underwear and was in the process of pulling up his trousers. He dropped his trousers to the floor and stood paralyzed, staring at the surprised congregation. Then, he picked up a nearby chair and held it in front of him.

"Do something quick!" one of the deacons shouted. So, a thoughtful deacon ran to the back and turned off all the lights, thinking that the man would take the hint to get dressed in the darkness.

Five minutes later when the lights were turned back on, the man was still standing there in his longhandled underwear, protecting himself with the chair. The lady, still gurgling and bubbling in the water, was fighting the curtains. The young pastor, in shock, was standing in the corner of the baptistry with his arms folded and his eyes staring straight ahead!

Four-year-old Jill, the pastor's daughter, had come up in the church, first going to the nursery and then to children's church. The first time she visited "big church," she witnessed her dad conducting a baptismal service. She almost shivered as she saw people being dunked under the water. Her mom explained that dad was "baptizing."

On Monday night Jill, crying uncontrollably, ran into her dad's home study. "Daddy, Daddy," she screamed, "Jimmy's upstairs baptizing my best doll!"

Several years ago an oil company had as its advertising slogan: "Put a tiger in your tank." Well, one Sunday a rather dogmatic preacher was baptizing.

The first candidate stepped into the water, and the preacher asked him, "Sir, are you a tither?"

The man replied, "Yes, but why do you ask now?"

Came the answer, "Because I want to put a *tither* in my tank!"

One preacher was baptizing an elderly woman who was deathly frightened about going beneath the water. The woman struggled as the preacher tried to put her under. The whole time she clung to the side of the baptistry with her right hand.

After the service the preacher met the woman in the vestibule, commenting, "Dear lady, if I believed in baptismal regeneration, I would have to consign your right hand to perdition."

After coming out of the water, a new member exclaimed, "Good grief, Preacher, I forgot to remove my wallet from these trousers. It's dripping wet."

"Hallelujah," exulted the preacher. "We could stand more baptized wallets."

Bible

The parson had been disturbed by a person who was a fast reader.

"We shall now read the Twenty-third Psalm in unison," he announced. "Will the lady who is always 'by the still waters' while the rest of us are 'in green pastures,' please wait a minute until we catch up?"

A Fugitive Found

Feeling footloose and frisky, a feather-brained fellow forced his fond father to fork over the farthings and flew far to foreign fields and frittered his fortune feasting fabulously with faithless friends.

Fleeced by his fellows in folly and facing famine, he found himself a feed flinger in a filthy farm. Fairly famishing, he fain would have filled his frame with foraged food from fodder fragments. "Phooey, my father's flunkies fare far finer!"

The frazzled fugitive frankly faced facts. He fled forthwith to his family. Falling at his father's feet, he forlornly fumbled. "Father, I've flunked and fruitlessly forfeited family favor."

The farsighted father, forstalling further flinching, frantically flagged the flunkies to fetch a fatling from the flock and fix a feast.

The fugitive's faultfinding brother frowned on fickle forgiveness of the former folderol.

But the faithful father figured, "Filial fidelity is fine, but the fugitive is found! What forbids fervent festivity? Let flags be unfurled! Let fanfares flair!"

Two girls walking home from Sunday School discussed a question suggested by a Bible passage. It was hearing the King James Version of the words that Jesus healed the sick "of divers diseases."

"I don't understand that part. What are 'divers diseases'?" asked the younger girl.

"What do you care what they are? You can't even swim," replied the more learned girl.

A woman parishioner demanded a house call by her pastor. He came, sat by her bed, and listened to her litany of woe. He counseled finally, "I think you will find help from some passages in the Bible which I wish to read to you."

In a syrupy voice she called to her little daughter playing in the next room, "Darling, bring mother that old book she loves so much."

Promptly the little girl brought in a copy of a popular movie-TV magazine.

Two small children were talking when the first asked the second one, "What kind of lights did Noah's ark have?"

The second child said, "I don't know. What kind?"

"Floodlights," answered the first child.

Question: "Who was the most successful doctor in the Bible?"
Answer: "Job, because he had the most patience."

A minister was given a parking ticket. In police court, the judge asked if he had anything to say.

"Yes," the minister replied. "Blessed are the merciful for they shall obtain mercy."

The judge fined him fifty dollars and admonished him, "Go thou and sin no more."

Bill: "Who was the straightest man in the Bible?"
Bob: "Joseph, because Pharaoh made a *ruler* out of him."

Building Program

A man was painting the church building. Noticing that he would not have enough paint to finish, he added thinner. As the paint continued to run out, the painter added more and more thinner.

A rainstorm the next day washed away his paint job. The pastor met the painter on the job and demanded that he "repaint and thin no more!"

A young boy gazed in delight at the new stained glass windows on the Sunday his church dedicated a new building.

"Look! Cartoons!" he cried.

The crumbling, old church building needed remodeling, so the preacher made an impassioned appeal, looking directly at the richest man in town.

At the end of the message, the rich man stood up and announced, "Pastor, I will contribute one thousand dollars."

Just then, plaster fell from the ceiling and struck the rich man on the shoulder. He promptly stood again and shouted, "Pastor, I will increase my donation to five thousand dollars."

Before he could sit back down, plaster fell on him again, and again he virtually screamed, "Pastor, I will double my last pledge."

He sat down, and a larger chunk of plaster fell, hitting him on the head. He stood once more and hollered, "Pastor, I will give twenty thousand dollars!"

This prompted a deacon to shout, "Hit him again, Lord! Hit him again!"

An innovative building committee member convinced his church that the new education building should have suitable Scripture verses inscribed over the doors of the various departments.

Over the entrance to the Sanctuary was placed the biblical verse: "O worship the Lord."

Over the nursery entrance was the apostle Paul's words in 1 Corinthians 15:51: "We shall not all sleep, but we shall all be changed!"

Bulletins

Announcement: Youth choir cookout by the creek. Time of praise and sin-a-long!

From a church bulletin: "A new loudspeaker system has been installed in the church. It was given by one of our members in honor of his wife."

A minister preached on "An Honest Christian" following the choir special, "Steal Away."

A minister commented in his church bulletin: "I have learned that it does not make a sermon immortal to make it everlasting."

From a bulletin: "The church dinner was like Heaven. Many we expected to see were absent."

Announcement in bulletin on Senior Day: "Members of the senior class are not to pass out until the pastor finishes speaking."

Business Meetings

Nothing dies faster than a new idea in some church business meetings.

Advice to the Moderator
1. When in doubt, mumble
2. When in trouble, delegate
3. When in charge, ponder.

A country church was located so far out in the country that for many years there was no electricity. Finally, an enterprising company offered electricity to the area.

At one of the business meetings of the church, someone stood and said, "I make a motion that our church buy a chandelier."

The most cantankerous member of the church, who always voted "agin" anything for which everyone else voted, made the following plea: "I hope we don't vote to buy a chandelier. After thinking long and hard on this situation, I have come up with three reasons why we should forget about buying a chandelier. In the first place, if we bought a chandelier, nobody would know how to spell it. In the second place, nobody in this church knows how to play it. And, besides all that, we need lights!"

One lad, bored by long, laborious business sessions at his church, finally attended his first circus. He reported to his mother, "If I had gone to a circus first, I might never have wanted to go to a church business meeting again."

Camp

A group of boys at church camp were asked the meaning of an archangel. No one knew. Then, one boy ventured, "One of the angels that came out of the ark?"

Camp is where parents spend many dollars to have their children taught how to make fifteen- and twenty-five-cent items which cost three dollars each to make!

Overheard at church camp: "Is it true that shepherds have dirty socks?" asked a camper.
"What do you mean?" answered a counselor.
"I heard that the shepherds washed their socks by night" returned the camper.

A counselor asked a camper, "What is righteous indignation?"
He thought for a moment and said, "That's to get real mad and not cuss."

When church camp dismissed, a young camper went to the counselor. "What would you like?" asked the counselor.

"I'd like to know what we learned at camp this week."

"That's an odd question. Why do you want to know that?" asked the counselor.

"They always ask me that when I get home, and I wouldn't know how to answer," came back the camper.

"Now, children, you must never do anything in private that you wouldn't do in public," stated a counselor to his campers.

One of the kids yelled, "Hurray! No more baths."

Children

Son: "That problem you helped me with last night was all wrong, Dad."
Father: "All wrong, was it? Well, I'm sorry."
Son: "Don't worry about it. None of the other daddies got it right either."

A Sunday School teacher, driving his five-year-old daughter to church, began thinking aloud about the ideas he expected to present to his college class that morning.

Susie listened for a moment, then asked, "Daddy, are you talking with me or without me?"

The average little boy uses soap as though it were coming out of his allowance.

After church one Sunday morning, a seven-year-old boy and his nine-year-old sister were arguing.

"Sibling rivalry?" asked an armchair psychiatrist.

"No," replied the mother, "sible war!"

Bart: "I have some bad news and some good news."

Mother: "What's the bad news?"

Bart: "I haven't done very well on my report card."

Mother: "And what's the good news?"

Bart: "I'm one of the three wise men in the Christmas play."

"Mommy, Mommy, I made 100 today at school!"

"Oh, I'm so proud of you, tell me about it."

"Well, I made 50 in spelling, 30 in history, and 20 in English!"

The pastor was teaching a class of boys. His lesson was almost like a sermon. The story was about Philip and the eunuch. Anxious to impress the boys with the joy of becoming a Christian, he asked, "Why did the eunuch go on his way rejoicing?"

One boy answered promptly, "Because Philip quit preaching."

To keep children from listening to your conversation, direct it at them.

The Sunday School teacher was teaching a lesson on creation to a class of children.

"Now, children," she said, "Who can tell me what makes the flower spring from the seed?"

"God does it," answered one little girl, "but fertilizer helps."

A small boy's prayer: "Dear God, I hope You take care of Yourself. 'Cause if anything happens to You, we would all be in a terrible mess."

"Mommy," said little Heather, "did you ever see a cross-eyed bear?"

"Why no, Heather," chuckled her mother, "but why do you ask?"

"Well, in church this morning, we sang about the 'consecrated cross-eyed bear.'"

A young girl became a Christian in an exciting revival at her church and was baptized the closing Sunday morning. That afternoon she ran through the house singing and dancing.

Her sour grandfather rebuked her with these words, "You ought to be ashamed of yourself. Just joined the church and singing and dancing on the Lord's Day!"

Crushed by her grandfather's attitude, the little girl went out to the barn, climbed up on the corral fence, and observed an old mule standing there with a sad, droopy face and bleary eyes.

As she reached over and patted the mule sympathetically, she said, "Don't cry, ole mule. I guess you've just got the same kind of religion that Grandpa has!"

Choirs

If our baritones were less barren and our tenors more tenable, we'd have less heterogeneous harmony and more mellifluous melody.

A little girl visited in a large church for the first time. She was surprised to see the choir members enter the sanctuary wearing choir robes and whispered in dismay to her mother, "They're not all going to preach, are they?"

Question: What was Noah's favorite country record?
Answer: "I Love a Rainy Night."

A large metropolitan church literally revolved around its music program. It was plain to see that music was the number one priority of this particular church.

At a business meeting, each member of the staff took his or her turn expressing their displeasure with their meager salaries which were being sacrificed at the altar of the church's music program.

Music was so popular in the church that, as each staff member spoke, he did so in a musical chant.

The janitor stood first and chanted to the congregation, "I'm the janitor of this church, and I make just $10,000 a year, and I want to say—THAT'S NOT MUCH TO LIVE ON!"

The secretary of the church stood and said, "I'm the secretary of this church, and I make just $5,000 a year, and I want to say—I DON'T GET PAID ENOUGH!"

The pastor stood and said, "I'm the pastor of this church, and I make just $20,000 a year, and I want to say—I COULD SURE USE MORE MONEY!"

Then, the music director stood and there was a fanfare played by the church orchestra. He cleared his voice and boomed loudly, "I'm the music director of this church, and I make $70,000 a year, and I just want to say— THERE'S NO BUSINESS LIKE SHOW BUSINESS!"

And the choir sang a sevenfold "AMEN!"

New Choir Member: "What is your position in the choir?"
Seasoned Singer: "Absolutely neutral, I don't side with either faction."

A church had a man in the choir who could not sing. Several people hinted to him that he could serve in other places, but he continued to come to the choir. The choir director became desperate and went to the pastor.

"You've got to get that man out of the choir," he said. "If you don't, I'm going to resign. The choir members are going to quit too. Please do something."

So the pastor went to the man and suggested, "Perhaps you should leave the choir."

"Why should I get out of the choir?" he asked.

"Well, five or six people have told me you can't sing."

"That's nothing," the man snorted. "Fifty people have told me that you can't preach!"

Mother: "What are you children playing?"
Children: "Church."
Mother: "But people shouldn't whisper in church."
Children: "We know, but we're in the choir!"

The choir was proud both of its precision in singing and of its dignified entrance down the long center aisle of the church. This church was heated by a furnace located in the basement. There was a large air grill in the center of the main aisle. During the week something had fallen through the grill, and the caretaker had removed it to retrieve the object. But in replacing it, he forgot to fasten it down.

As the choir entered, the sopranos stepped carefully over the iron grill.

An alto forgot, stepped on it, and caught her high heel in the grill. With great presence of mind she stepped out of her shoe and, not missing a beat, continued down the aisle.

The tenor behind her saw what had happened. He reached down, still singing, and picked up her shoe. The whole grill came with it, but he didn't miss a note as he continued down the aisle, clutching shoe and grill.

The bass behind him didn't notice any of this. With quiet dignity, he stepped into the open hole and disappeared into the basement.

A soprano who sang in a choir
Soared earnestly higher and higher,
Till her uppermost note
Got stuck in her throat
And lifted her clear through the spire.

Committees

A pastor search committee inquired of a prospective preacher, "Why did you leave your last church?"

He replied, "Sickness and fatigue! Church members were sick of me and I was tired of being their pastor!"

Question: What do a game of golf and a committee meeting have in common?
Answer: You go around and around for hours and end up where you started.

Committee Laws
1. Never arrive on time, or you will be labeled a beginner.
2. Don't say anything until the meeting is half over; this makes you appear to be wise.
3. Be as vague as possible; this prevents irritating others.
4. When in doubt, suggest that a subcommittee be appointed.
5. Be the first to move for adjournment; this will make you popular—it's what everyone is waiting for.

A lady in church wondered why everybody was criticizing a certain committee. She said, "They haven't done a thing!"

Seeing his first American football game, the Englishman watched one of the teams go into a huddle.

"What do you think of football?" asked his friend.

"It's not a bad sport," he answered, "but they have too many committee meetings."

One reason the Ten Commandments are so brief and concise is that they didn't come through a committee.

Complaints and Compliments

Two worldly men saw an elderly churchgoer coming down the street. One man pointed toward her.

"I'll bet you can't mention anybody that old Miss Thompson can't find something good to say about."

The other fellow called the bet.

"Good morning, Miss Thompson," he said politely. "What do you think about the devil?"

Miss Thompson cocked her perky little head over to one side. "Well," she answered, "there is one good thing about him. He is always on the job."

Don was taking the civil service test to become a mailcarrier. The first question was, "How far is the earth from the moon?"

"Look," he said to the examiner, "if that's gonna be my route—you can forget it!"

The pastor missed his plane, stood there looking at his watch, then angrily drove back to town with it and stopped at the jewelry store operated by his parishioner.

"I had faith in this watch," he told the jeweler, "but it has failed me."

The jeweler inspected the watch, then said, "Well, Pastor, you should know that 'faith without works is dead.'"

Pastor to church hostess: "How did this fly get in my soup?"
Hostess: "I guess it flew in, sir."
Pastor: "What's he doing in my soup?"
Hostess: "Looks like the backstroke to me!"

A very wise old minister had kept on his desk for over a half-century a notebook labeled "Complaints of Members." Whenever any member of his church came in to complain about somebody else's conduct, the old pastor would nod and pick up the notebook, saying, "Thank you, I'll just write it down so I can take it up officially with the church board."

The book and the poised pen worked. The opportunity was offered hundreds of times, but nothing was ever written in the book.

A young man stood to preach his first sermon. He was so frightened that he could hardly speak. He had written a good, long sermon, however, so he just kept plodding on through it.

"Speak up!" a man yelled from the back of the church. "We can't hear you back here!"

The young man tried to preach louder. Yet in a little while the man called out again, "We can't hear you!"

The young man tried a little harder, but he became more frightened by the minute. Finally, the man in the back stood up. "We can't hear a thing you are saying!"

Another churchgoer in the front stood up, turned around, and asked, "What are you complaining about? Just sit down and thank God, or I will change places with you."

A church member told her pastor that his sermons on television meant so much more to her husband since he had lost his mind.

A church in the conference asked for a new minister every year. In this same conference, they had a minister who asked for a new church every year. The bishop decided to assign the minister who wanted another church each year to the church that wanted a new minister every year. To his surprise, for three years there was no request.

"I don't understand," commented the bishop to a member of the church. "You always wanted a new preacher every year until this preacher came—you have had him three years. How do you account for that?"

One of the members said, "Bishop, if you really want to know—our church didn't want no preacher to start with, and this man you sent us is the nearest thing to 'no preacher' we ever had!"

Confusion

A drunk man on his way home was walking across a church lawn. He came to a young tree with a picket fence around it. He felt his way around the fence four or five times and then sat down.

"Now I am in trouble," he moaned, "I'm fenced in at the church."

During the first day at Sunday School the teacher informed all of the students that if anyone had to go to the restroom, he or she should raise a hand.

"How's that going to help?" asked one lad.

Most churches need three monkeys—one who sees no upheaval, one who hears no upheaval, and another who speaks no upheaval.

A young minister was delivering one of his first sermons in his first pastorate. Excited and wishing to make a good impression, he became confused about a scriptural event.

"Consider the scene where the Master fed the multitude with five thousand loaves and two thousand fishes." A visitor shook his head in a vigorous "No!"

Wishing to correct his error, the young preacher began his next Sunday's sermon with the words: "Consider the scene where the Master fed five thousand people with five loaves and two fishes." He pointed to the visitor and emphasized, "You couldn't do that, brother!"

"Oh yes, I could," said the man, "I could if I had what was left over last Sunday!"

"I can't decide whether to become a Moose, an Elk, or a Lion," the new pastor said *gamely*.

"Let's burn down Rome."

"There's no need to do that—rumor has it that Nero is going to do it himself someday."

"Let's not wait on Nero to do it. Let's go ahead and burn it down ourselves—that way we will eliminate the fiddle man!"

A man was a member of a church where the members were having a lot of difficulty. He became so nervous that he couldn't speak. He went to the doctor, and the doctor gave him some tranquilizers.

Two days later he went back to the doctor and asked, "Doctor, what did you give me?"

He replied, "I gave you some tranquilizers."

"Well, I don't want any more of them."

The doctor asked, "Why not?"

He replied, "They made me act friendly with people I don't like at church."

A little girl sitting in church with her father suddenly felt ill.

"Daddy," she whispered, "I have to vomit!"

Her father told her to hurry to the restroom.

In less than two minutes the child was back. "I didn't have to go too far," she exclaimed. "There's a little box by the door that says, 'For the sick.'"

Deacons, Elders, and Stewards

The pastor had just come to a new church. He was talking to one of the deacons and the deacon said, "Pastor, we have been talking among ourselves about what to call you."

The pastor said, "What did you call the last pastor?"

The deacon replied, "We called him the 'Hog Caller.'"

The pastor looked a little surprised and said, "At the last place, they called me the 'Shepherd of the Flock,' but of course you know your own people here better than I do."

A deacon and his wife were in the dry cleaning business. He worked on the same spot for ten years.

Two deacons were out hunting and came upon a game warden. He reminded them that if they became lost to fire a shot at 4:00 P.M. He added that, if not found by a search party by 4:30 P.M., another shot should be fired, and also one at 5:00 P.M.

Sure enough, that afternoon they realized they were lost. At the appointed times they fired their shots. Said one, "If we aren't found soon, we'll run out of arrows."

A deacon was presenting the congregation's gift to a pastor about to leave for other duties. "He was a diligent visitor among his people," asserted the speaker, "and many homes were happy when he left."

A Baptist deacon had advertised a cow for sale.

"How much are you asking for it?" inquired a prospective buyer.

"A hundred and fifty dollars," replied the advertiser.

"And how much milk does she give?"

"Four gallons a day," he replied.

"But how do I know she'll actually give that amount?" asked the purchaser.

"Oh, you can trust me," he explained, "I'm a Baptist deacon."

"I'll buy it," answered the other. "I'll take the cow home and bring back the money later. You can trust me, I'm a Presbyterian elder."

When the deacon arrived home, he asked his wife, "What's a Presbyterian elder?"

"Oh," she explained, "a Presbyterian elder is about the same as a Baptist deacon."

"Oh, dear," groaned the deacon, "I've lost my cow."

A teenage boy was asked to explain the meaning of a bishop, priest, and deacon.

He answered, "I never saw a bishop, so I don't know. A priest is a man in the Old Testament. A deacon is a thing that sits along the seashore and blinks at night."

Epitaphs

A fellow was out in the cemetery reading epitaphs on the tombstones. He came to one that read, "Not dead, but sleeping."

He shook his head. "Man, you're not fooling anybody but yourself."

Epitaph on a dentist's tombstone: "Filling my last cavity."

What's the "Voice of the graves?"
"Tomb's Tone."

Question: What did they put on the cabinet-maker's stone?
Answer: "Here lies a counter-fitter."

Inscription on the monument of an army mule: "In memory of Kate, who in her time kicked a colonel, three majors, eight captains, twelve lieutenants, twenty-one sergeants, 230 others, and one bomb."

A tombstone reads: "Excuse me for not rising."

On a Pastor's Monument
> *Go tell the Church that I am
>   dead,*
> *But they need shed no tears;*
> *For though I'm dead I'm no more
>   dead*
> *Than they have been for years.*

Epitaph in a dog cemetery: "He never met a man he didn't lick."

Funerals, Death

A funeral director called a man for further instructions about his mother-in-law's body.

"Do you want her embalmed, cremated, or buried?" he asked.

"All three!" the man answered promptly. "Don't take any chances."

A fellow had just laid a wreath of flowers on a friend's grave. While crossing another section of the cemetery he saw an Oriental man lay some rice on the grave of a family friend.

"When do you expect your friend to come and eat that rice?" asked the fellow.

"When your friend comes to smell the flowers," he answered.

A Baptist family had a death in the family while their minister was out of town. They asked the local Methodist minister to conduct the funeral service.

He called his bishop and asked, "Can I bury a Baptist?"

The bishop quickly replied, "Sure, bury all the Baptists you can!"

There was a rule in a small community that no one would be buried until someone offered to speak a good word about the deceased. The most ungodly man in the community died, and no one offered to say a word for him.

At last the man's neighbor offered to speak a word for him, So arrangements were made for the funeral. The whole community attended to hear what in the world this man would say. When the crowd had assembled, the neighbor stood up.

"Well," he drawled, "I remember that sometimes Old Bill wasn't as bad as he was most of the time."

A dear old lady knew her time of final departure was approaching.

"Soon, I'll be rocking in the bosom of Moses," she told her pastor.

"No, dear," said the pastor, "the Bible says the bosom of Abraham."

"At my age, you don't care too much whose bosom it is!"

Future Life

Preacher: "Do you want to go to heaven?"
Unbeliever: "No, sir."
Preacher: "Of course you want to go to heaven when you die."
Unbeliever: "Oh sure, when I die. I thought you were organizing a group to go today."

A doctor was teaching a Sunday School class of boys. The lesson was about heaven. He wanted to impress upon them the importance of becoming Christians so they could go to heaven.

"Now, what do you have to do before you can go to heaven?"

One boy's hand shot up, and the doctor called on him.

"Get sick and call for you," he answered.

"My boy," asked his boss, "do you believe in life after death?"

"Yes, sir."

"Then that makes everything just fine," his employer continued tenderly. "About an hour after you left yesterday to attend your grandfather's funeral, he came in to see you."

A mother commented, "If heaven's a place of rest, my teenage son's going to be practiced up for it."

A very rich and very wicked old man was dying. He seemed so worried that his family asked the pastor to come and comfort him.

"I wouldn't mind dying so much," the old man said, "if I could take my money with me and keep it safe."

"Don't worry about that," the preacher replied. "It'll all be burned up anyway."

"Mama, don't men ever go to heaven?" asked a small boy.

His mother answered, "Of course they do! What makes you ask?"

"Because I never saw any pictures of angels with whiskers."

"Oh, that's because most men who go to heaven get there by a close shave!"

The teacher smiled at her Sunday School group and exclaimed, "All right, class, all those who want to go to heaven raise your hands."

Everybody in the class had a hand raised, except one boy. "Don't you want to go to heaven?" asked the teacher.

"I can't, ma'am. My mom wants me to come straight home."

Four philosophers were discussing world salvation. Commented one, "Now if we could just eliminate all profanity, this would be a better world."

Opined another, "If we could eliminate all liquor, we would have a better world."

Remarked a third, "If we could get rid of those and all other sinful things, we would have the millennium."

At which point the fourth philosopher growled, "Yes, and then we would have *that* to put up with!"

A three-year-old said to his father when it was raining, "I don't think heaven's such a nice place at all."

"Why not?" asked his father.

"Because," he answered, "the floor is all full of holes and lets the water through."

A college bulletin board read: "The end of the world has been postponed until next semester due to a shortage of harps and trumpets."

A politician was approached by an irate voter. He insulted the man running for office, "I wouldn't vote for you if you were St. Peter himself."

"If I were St. Peter," snapped back the candidate, "you couldn't vote for me. You wouldn't be in my district!"

Gossip

The preacher overheard this talk between two men in the church hallway: "Listen carefully, because I can only tell this once. I promised not to repeat it."

Gossip is information given by someone who can't use it, to someone who won't.

Some people will believe anything if they happen to overhear it.

It's all right to hold a conversation, but you should let go of it now and then.

The time had come for the funeral of a woman who always kept her church and community in an uproar with her gossip. It was a dark, stormy day, and the lights were on in the chapel. The preacher was quietly conducting the service.

Suddenly a bolt of lightning shook the building and the lights went out. The preacher stopped talking, and, in the sudden stillness, a voice was heard from the audience.

"She got there!"

Believe only half of what you hear, but be sure it's the right half.

A rumor goes in one ear and out many mouths.

Secret: Something which is hushed about from place to place.

Gossip seems to travel faster over sour grapevines.

Hospitals

A minister called at the home of a member when he learned he was seriously ill in the hospital.

"Oh, he's improving," said the wife, "but he's still in the *expensive-care* ward."

Patient: "I think my nurse used to be a mail-carrier. When I came back from the operation, she shoved me under the door."

The Gown with the Split Down the Back
> *I was sittin' here mindin' my business,*
> *Kinda lettin' my mind go slack,*
> *When in comes a nurse with a bright, sunny smile*
> *And a gown that was split down the back.*
>
> *"Take a shower," she said, "and get ready,*
> *And then jump into this sack."*
> *What she was really talkin' about*
> *Was the gown with the split down the back.*

"They're coming to do some tests,"
    she said.
They're gonna stretch me out on a
    rack,
With nothin' twixt me and the
    cold, cruel world,
But a gown that's split down the
    back!

It comes only to the knees in
    front,
In the sides there is also a lack,
But by far the greatest shortcom-
    ing
Is that bloomin' split down the
    back.

Whoever designed this garment,
For humor had a great knack.
But I fail to see anything funny
'Bout a gown that's split down
    the back.

I hear them coming to get me,
The wheels going clickety-clack.
I'll ride through the halls on a
    table,
In a gown with a split down the
    back!

*When I get to heaven it'll make
  me no odds
If my robe is white, red, or black.
The only thing I will ask is,
  "Please,
Give me one with no split down
  the back."*

A hospital room is a place where friends of the patient go to talk to other friends of the patient.

A boy came home after his first day in Sunday School and told his mother that the teacher asked him where he was born.

"You said the hospital, didn't you?" asked his mother.

"Nah. I didn't wanna sound like a sissy, so I said the Superdome!"

One thing not to say in a hospital is: "You look fine. I hardly recognized you at all."

A surgeon was discussing a forthcoming operation with a wealthy patient.

"Would you prefer a local anesthetic?" he inquired.

"I can afford the best," replied the wealthy patient. "Get something imported."

An expectant mother was being rushed to the hospital but didn't quite make it. Instead, she gave birth to her baby on the hospital lawn. Later, the father received a bill listing: "Delivery room fee, $500." He wrote the hospital and reminded them that the baby was born on the front lawn.

A week later, he received a corrected bill reading: "Greens' fee, $200."

He was making his first visit to a hospital where his teenage son was about to have an operation. Watching the doctor's every move, he asked, "What's that?"

The doctor explained, "This is an anesthetic; after he gets this he won't know a thing."

"Save your time, Doc," exclaimed the man, "He don't know anything now."

Two men were sitting in the expectant fathers' lounge at a hospital. A nurse walked over to one and said, "Congratulations. You have a little daughter."

The other man leaped up and shouted, "Hey, that ain't fair. I was here first!"

Lord's Supper, Communion

The young pastor was on two "honeymoons." He had just married, and he and his new bride had moved to their first pastorate. Their first home was the parsonage located next door to the church building.

The deacons announced, "Pastor, on your first Sunday night as our pastor we have planned to have the Lord's Supper." It was his responsibility to prepare the elements for the Lord's Supper service. So on Sunday afternoon, he and his wife poured the grape juice into the little cups and prepared the unleavened bread for what would be his first experience of administering the Lord's Supper.

It was an unusually large crowd that night. As the deacons served the juice, the young pastor stood reverently at the front of the church observing the congregation. Suddenly, it occurred to him that the crowd was larger than the number of juice containers.

He leaned over the front row and whispered to his wife, "We are going to run out of grape juice!"

"What do you want me to do?" asked his anxious bride.

"Run next door to the parsonage and get that bottle of grape juice out of the refrigerator. If you run fast enough, you can be back here by the time the deacons get back down the aisle."

The pastor's wife bolted out the side door of the church into the kitchen of the parsonage next door. She didn't bother to switch on the lights. She rushed to the refrigerator, reached in, and got what she thought was a bottle of grape juice. But it was not a bottle of grape juice. It was a bottle of green persimmon juice!

In the midst of the emergency, neither she nor her husband bothered to read the label. Frantically, she handed the bottle to her young husband/pastor. He uncapped it and poured its contents into the small juice containers for himself and the deacons.

It was like clockwork! Just as he had finished filling the cups for himself and the deacons, the deacons were reverently marching down the aisle with empty trays after having served the congregation.

The pastor picked up the tray of juice glasses and slowly served his deacons. Then, he led the whole congregation in drinking the juice.

Suddenly strange things began to happen. The young pastor's lips began to pucker. He knew he was in trouble.

"Deacon Jones," he wheezed, "will you please lead us in the closing prayer?"

Deacon Jones was having his own problems with the persimmon juice. He smacked his lips and barely managed to say, "Pastor, please excuse me!"

The pastor surveyed the situation and called on Deacon Smith to lead in the closing prayer. Deacon Smith made some funny noises through his puckered lips and begged to be excused from leading the closing prayer.

The young pastor turned to the bewildered congregation, motioned for them to stand, and said, "Well, friends, let's all stand, whistle the Doxology, and go home!"

Missionaries

A missionary heard about a native who had five wives.

"You are violating a law of God," said the good missionary. "You must go and tell four of those women they can no longer live here or consider you their husband."

The native thought a few moments, then said, "Me wait here. You tell 'em."

A missionary visiting a cannibal tribe asked the chief, "Do you people know anything about religion?"

"Well," explained the chief, "we got a little taste of it when the last missionary was here."

A missionary, deep in the jungle, came upon a witch doctor who was pounding heavily on a drum.

"What is going on?" asked the frightened missionary.

"We have no water," explained the native.

"I see," said the religious leader. "So you're praying for rain?"

"No," said the witch doctor, "I'm sending for the plumber."

After the service the little boy lingered behind and insisted on seeing the missionary.

"Ah, my lad," said the kindly missionary as he patted the boy's head, "do you wish to consecrate your young life to this noble work?"

"No, sir," replied the boy, "I want to know if you've got any foreign stamps."

Money

With all this inflation going on, about all you can get for a dollar is a picture of George Washington.

A boss asked an employee, "Why were you trying to go over my head for a raise?"

The employee denied it, saying, "I did not!"

The boss then asked, "You were praying for a raise, weren't you?"

Did you hear about the woman who told the bank teller: "I want to make this withdrawal from my husband's half of our joint account."

The minister asked, "Is there anybody in the congregation who wants a prayer said for their shortcomings?"

"Yes," was the answer from a man in the front pew. "I'm a spendthrift. I throw money around like it is growing on trees!"

"Very well," said the minister. "We will join in prayer for our brother—just as soon as the collection plates have been passed."

Pastor's Wife: "If you were rich, what would you want most of all?"
Pastor: "An alarm clock with a busted buzzer."

A minister received a call from the Internal Revenue Service asking about a member of his church.

"He stated on his income tax return," said the official, "that he gave three thousand dollars last year to your church. Is that correct?"

"I don't have the records here, and I would have to check on it. But I'll say this—if he didn't, he will."

It's odd the number of folks walking around with pocket calculators and next to nothing in their pockets to calculate.

The minister had a special filing drawer for his bills. It was labeled: "Due unto Others."

A wife woke up her husband and told him a burglar was going through his pants pockets.

His reply was, "Let me go to sleep. You two argue over who gets the contents."

A minister told his congregation, "So now let us give freely, generously, in accordance with what you reported on your income tax."

On Sunday morning a father gave his son a fifty-cent piece and a dollar.

"Put the dollar in the offering," the father said. "Then you can have the fifty cents for ice cream."

When the boy came home he still had the dollar.

"Why didn't you put the dollar in the offering?" his father asked.

"Well, it was like this," the boy answered. "The preacher said God loves a cheerful giver. I could give the fifty-cent piece a lot more cheerfully than I could the dollar."

People today are chiefly concerned about the higher things of life-like prices.

The pastor, after preaching an eloquent stewardship sermon, was going from the pulpit to the altar when an enthusiastic lady, extremely moved by his sermon, put a coin into his hand, saying, "I must give my mite," to which he replied, looking at the coin, "I thought there were supposed to be two of them."

A man fell into a lake, and a friend pulled him out.

"You should give your friend at least twenty dollars for saving your life," suggested the man's minister.

The man replied, "Could I make it ten dollars, Pastor? I was half dead when he pulled me out."

"I've been racking my brain, but I can't place you," one man said to another at a gathering. "And you look very much like somebody I have seen a lot—somebody I don't like but I can't tell you why. Isn't that strange?"

"Nothing strange about it," the other man said. "You have seen me a lot, and I know why you resent me. For two years I have passed you the collection plate in our church!"

Several "Up-East" counterfeiters accidentally printed a batch of fifteen-dollar bills. Moe asked Joe, "Man, what we gonna do with all dese fifteen-dollar bills?"

Joe came up with a bright idea, "I got it. We'll drive down to hillbilly country and pawn these bills off on the storekeepers back in the mountains."

Hours later they pulled up to a dilapidated store on the side of a mountain. Moe and Joe winked at each other. They found the old proprietor sitting by the potbellied stove.

Moe ambled over to the elderly gent and nonchalantly asked, "Hey, mister, can you make change for a fifteen-dollar bill?"

Without batting an eyelash the proprietor inquired, "How do you want it, sonny? Five threes or a seven and an eight?"

Optimism and Pessimism

"Helpful" Counselor: "I believe one out of every four people in the United States is mentally unbalanced. Think of that . . . one out of every four. You don't have to take my word for it; you can prove this for yourself. Here's what I want you to do. Think of three of your best friends. Do they seem all right to you? Because if they do, you must be the one."

An optimist is a man who marries his secretary and thinks he'll be able to continue dictating to her.

Applying for a secretarial position at the church, the young lady came to the question "Marital status," and she replied without hesitation: "hopeful."

A sad-looking fellow was sitting before his minister, who was trying to help him. "You say that you've failed in every business you've tried?" the good preacher asked. "You speak only of failure."

"That's right," the man nodded, eyes downcast.

"Well, now!" the minister spoke heartily. "I say to you, sir, that you must get the power of positive thinking. You must forget failure and think positively, never negatively. You can start right now. Will you do that?"

"Yes, sir," the man nodded, showing a spark of life. "I see what you mean. I now know positively I am going to fail again."

Optimist: happychondriac.

"You can always find something good to say about people if you try real hard."

A boy had heard his pastor make this truism. The fellow had just started the third grade and was not fond of his teacher, but he determined to think of something nice to say to her.

"Miss Jones," he said one morning, "you're the best third grade teacher I ever had."

Righteous Indignation: jealousy with a halo.

A town was hit by a bomb, leaving only two Baptist preachers and two Baptist deacons. Immediately they organized a church and set a goal for six the next Sunday.

A pessimist is a person who, when there is a choice of two evils, takes both.

An optimist can have more fun guessing wrong than a pessimist can have guessing right.

How you can spot a pessimist: He turns out the light to see how dark it is.

Pastors, Priests, and Rabbis

A man came along the road to find a friend lying in the ditch where he had been knocked after being hit by a truck. As he lay on his back groaning, the rain came pouring down, and lightning flashed about him. "Get me a rabbi. Get me a rabbi," called the victim.

"Are you mad? You're a Catholic, and what would you want a rabbi for?" asked his friend.

The victim opened his eyes reproachfully, "Aw, who would think of asking a priest to come out on a night like this?"

A young preacher looked up from his reading and inquired of his wife, "How many great preachers do you think there are?"

She answered, "I don't know, but there is one less than you think!"

An old Scottish guide was a devoutly religious man—and a lover of good hunting. On one occasion he returned from a shooting trip with the new minister and sank wearily into his chair.

"Here's a cup o' hot tea for ye," said his devoted spouse. "And is the new minister a good shot?"

The guide reflected for a moment. It was strictly against his principles to speak a disparaging word about a man of the cloth. At length he made his response. "Aye, old woman," he said. "Aye, a fine shot he is—but 'tis marvelous how the Lord protects the birds when he's shooting!"

Everything in football has become so specialized. Whenever one Catholic school travels they take two priests with them—the defensive chaplain and the offensive chaplain.

A pastor asked a boy, "What is the Trinity?"

The boy had a weak voice and answered somewhat quietly, "Father, Son, and Holy Spirit."

Commented the pastor, "I can't understand you."

To which the bright young Christian replied, "You're not supposed to—it's a mystery!"

A priest was listening to a young man confess his sins. He stopped him and said, "Wait a minute, young man; you aren't confessing— you're bragging!"

A noted clergyman was asked why the loud, shouting messages of his earlier days had given way to a more quiet, persuasive manner of speech.

"When I was young," he replied, "I thought it was the thunder that killed people, but as I grew older I discovered it was lightning. So I determined that in the future I would thunder less and lightnin' more!"

The rabbi finally decided he must talk to the richest member of his congregation, no matter how much it hurt.

"Why," asked the rabbi, "do you fall asleep when I'm delivering my message?"

Answered the rich man, "Would I fall asleep if I didn't trust you?"

The story goes: There is a chain letter making the rounds among the churches these days in which no cost is involved. You merely send a copy of the letter to six other churches that are tired of their ministers. Then you bundle up your pastor and send him to the church at the bottom of the list. In one week you will receive 16,436 ministers, and one of them should be a dandy. But beware—one church broke the chain and got their old minister back!

A Catholic priest and a Methodist minister were driving rather rapidly down a country road headed to the golf course. The priest ran over a rabbit that was playing in the road. He stopped the car, took a vial out of the glove compartment, and said to his companion, "I am really very sorry I did that. At least I can give the poor creature the last rites." Whereupon he anointed the prone rabbit with holy water.

The Methodist then took a bottle out of his golf bag and sprinkled some of its contents on the apparently lifeless bunny. Immediately, the rabbit came to life, jumped into the air, and in a moment had run across a nearby field.

The priest was astonished. "I didn't know you Methodists used such potent holy water," he remarked.

"We don't," replied the minister. "That was hare restorer."

Atheist: A fellow playing golf with a minister, a priest, and a rabbi who won't concede a two-inch putt.

A minister answered his telephone to hear a woman's voice request, "Send six cases of vodka to my house, please."

The pastor recognized the voice as that of one of his parishioners. Gently he replied, "I am your minister."

He expected an apology by her for dialing the wrong number. Instead she retorted almost angrily, "What are you doing at the liquor store?"

Trying to comfort a member upon his resigning, the pastor said, "But, my dear, it's likely that the next pastor will be far better than I've been."

She remained inconsolable and said, "That's what they said the last time."

A traffic cop flagged down a young driver, got his name, then snarled, "Oh, so you're a preacher, hey? Now don't go telling me you didn't see that stop sign."

Alibied the minister, "Oh, to be sure I saw the sign, Officer. The point is—I didn't see you."

An ecstatic young minister wanted to tell his parents about his new baby boy and that his wife was in good health. So he telegraphed his mother this message: "Isaiah 9:6."

Mom got the message . . . partially. She telephoned her husband at his office and said: "A telegram came. Our son's wife evidently had a boy who weighs nine pounds and six ounces, and they have named him Isaiah."

Picnics, Fellowships

A fellow went to a church fellowship with both of his ears bright red.

A friend asked him, "What did you do to your ears?"

"Terrible thing," said the fellow. "While I was ironin' my shirt to come tonight, the phone rang, and well, I picked up the iron instead of the phone."

"That's so gross," said the friend sympathetically, "but, what happened to the other ear?"

"The same guy called back!"

It was the annual summer gathering of the local ministerial alliance. Every denomination in the city was represented by one or more ministers as they gathered in a meeting room of a motel.

In the next room, the local brewery association was having its "summer fling."

Both groups were to be served large slices of fresh watermelon. The brewery association had requested that their watermelons be "spiked" with "appropriate spirits."

The head waiter at the restaurant made a mortal mistake! He accidently switched the watermelons, and the ministers ended up with the "spiked" watermelons; however, he discovered his mistake too late.

He went to the manager and asked, "What shall I do?" The manager advised, "Well, the best thing to do, at this point, is to survey the situation and let me know what's happening."

In a few minutes the waiter returned to his manager and made the following report, "Sir, it's too late to do anything about it. They've already eaten the watermelons!"

"Well, what are they doing now?" asked the manager.

The exasperated waiter reported as follows: "The Catholic priest has collected little chunks of watermelon, and he is squeezing them through a handkerchief into a glass and sipping the juice slowly. The Jewish rabbi is trying to buy an extra watermelon to carry home. The Episcopalian rector is gnawing on a rind. The Methodist minister is demanding seconds, and the Baptist minister is going from plate to plate collecting seeds!"

Prayers

A little boy prayed, "Lord, if you can't make me a better boy, don't worry about it. I'm having a real good time like I am!"

Up near the dangerous front, an Army chaplain was conducting worship services. Artillery explosions were heard nearby, right in the middle of the chaplain's prayer. He paused in mid-sentence and spoke louder, "Is that outgoing or incoming?"

Together the reverent soldiers answered, "Outgoing, sir."

The chaplain reverently resumed his prayer right in the middle of the sentence where he had stopped.

Many of us need the prayer of the old saint who prayed, "Lord, keep me alive while I'm still living."

Seven-year-old George came out with a loud, shrill whistle during the minister's prayer one Sunday.

After church, his mother scolded him and asked, "Son, whatever made you do such a thing?"

"I asked God to teach me to whistle, and He did just then," answered the boy.

Minister: "So your mother says your prayers for you each night? What does she say?"

"Thank God, he's in bed!"

Just before the football game started, both teams gathered together and prayed briefly. A fan seated next to a rabbi asked what he thought would happen if both teams prayed with equal faith and fervor.

"In that event," replied the rabbi, "I imagine the Lord would simply sit back and enjoy one fine game of football."

Television prayer: "Lord, comfort those who are afflicted by the television today."

A four-year-old fashioned his prayer after what he thought he heard in church: "And forgive us our trashbaskets as we forgive those who put trash in our baskets."

Question: What do you get when you cross a praying mantis with a termite?

Answer: A bug that says grace before eating your house.

An elderly preacher is reported to have prayed the following prayer each day: "O Lord, give me a backbone as big as a saw log and ribs like the large timbers under the church floor. Put iron shoes on my feet and galvanized breeches on my body. Give me a rhinoceros hide for skin, and hang up a wagonload of determination in the gable-end of my soul. Help me to sign the contract to fight the devil as long as I've got a tooth—and then gum him until I die."

Devout golfer: One who prays with an interlocking grip.

A little girl whose father had refused a request said in her prayer that night: "And please don't give my parents any more children. They don't know how to treat the ones they've got."

Two men were shipwrecked. One of them started to pray, "Dear Lord, I've broken most of the Commandments. I've been an awful sinner all my days. Lord, if you'll spare me I'll—"

The other one shouted, "Hold on, don't commit yourself. I think I see a boat!"

How to say grace, with grace, when seated before the sole item of food on the table: a single beet.

"Dear God . . . that beet's all. Amen."

"Do you say your prayers at night, little boy?" inquired the preacher.

"Yes, sir," answered the lad.

"And do you always say them in the morning, too?"

"No, sir," responded the lad, "I ain't scared in the daytime."

A boy asked his politician father, "What does the chaplain of Congress do?"

The realistic dad replied, "He stands up, looks at the congressmen, and then prays for the country."

A small child attended church with his parents. When he knelt to say his prayers before going to bed, he prayed: "Dear Lord, we had a good time at church today. I wish You could have been there!"

An officer who had been overseas on an extended tour received a letter from his wife telling about a prayer their four-year-old daughter made: "Dear Lord, please send me a baby brother so we will have something to surprise Daddy with when he gets home."

The minister of a church discovered at the last minute that he hadn't invited a devoted elderly member to attend his garden party. He called and asked her to come on over.

"It's no use," she informed him. "I've already prayed for rain."

The pastor's morning prayer began, "O, Lord, give us clean hearts, give us pure hearts, give us sweet hearts," and every girl in the congregation fervently responded, "Ah-men!"

Preaching

*A young theologian named
    Twiddle
Refused to accept his degree.
He said, "It's bad enough being
    Twiddle,
Without being Twiddle, D.D."*

In the middle of a sermon, a man jumped up. "Brethren!" he shouted. "I have been a miserable, contemptible sinner for years, and never knew it before tonight!"

A deacon in the nearby pew announced, "Sit down, Brother. The rest of us knew it all the time."

Deacon: "How do you like the new pastor?"
Church Member: "Don't like him much. He preached so long I couldn't keep awake, and he hollered so loud I couldn't go to sleep."

Question: What is a minister doing when he rehearses his sermon?
Answer: Practicing what he preaches.

A pastor who had been having difficulties with his church accepted a chaplaincy at the state penitentiary. When he preached his farewell sermon at the church, he told his members why he was leaving.

"You don't love me," he moaned. "You haven't paid my salary. You don't love one another. I haven't had a wedding since I've been here. We haven't had a funeral in this church since I've been here. I'm going to be chaplain at the penitentiary. Now I will preach this morning on a text from John 14." He cleared his throat and read, "I go to prepare a place for you."

Then he announced the special number—"Meet Me There."

One thing a preacher should remember for sure: The mind can absorb only what the seat can endure.

A preacher's daughter, asked if her father ever preached the same sermon more than once, replied, "Yes, I think he does; but he hollers in different places."

A man visited a neighboring church and reported on the powerful sermon he heard. It was so moving that first he noted the children in tears, then the women cried, and finally even the men had moist eyes.

His friend inquired, "Did you cry too?"
He replied, "No, I'm not a member there."

A great old Baptist preacher/Bible expositor of years past was sometimes called "a long-winded preacher." Sometimes he preached as long as two hours, hurling his words like bursts of fire.

One morning he faced his congregation and said: "Some of you came today with thimbles to receive the water of the Word. You will get them full in about five minutes and then are free to leave. Those who brought spiritual teacups can stay a little longer, until they are full. If you brought quart bottles, it will take a little longer for me to fill them, and even longer to fill gallon buckets. But some of you came with barrels. You will be glad to stay until your barrels are full."

Poor Preaching: the art of expressing a two-minute idea with a one-hour vocabulary.

A preacher was writing a sermon, and his son asked, "Daddy, does the Lord tell you what to say?"

"Of course, He does!"

"Then why do you keep scratching some of it out?"

A preacher's little boy inquired, "Daddy, I notice every Sunday morning when you first come out to preach, you sit up on the platform and bow your head. What are you doing?"

The father explained, "I'm asking the Lord to give me a good sermon."

The little boy said, "Why don't He?"

One man inquired, "What color are your pastor's eyes?"

The person answered, "I don't know—when he prays he shuts his eyes and when he preaches I shut my eyes."

A cautious preacher concluded his sermon with the words: "The sinners referred to in my sermon are fictitious. Any similarity to members of this congregation is strictly coincidental!"

Revivals and Evangelists

The evangelist had preached for an hour and a half. Noticing the restlessness of his congregation, he asked, "Does anyone have a watch?"

A boy on the front row answered promptly, "Nope. But there's a calendar right in back of you."

A small country church was having a "baptizing" in a river on a cold January day. A revival meeting had just concluded. The preacher asked one baptismal candidate, "Is the water cold?"

"Naw!" he replied.

One of the deacons shouted, "Dip him again, Preacher; he's still lyin'!"

At the close of a service conducted by a famous evangelist, a woman came to him and was terribly upset. "I'll never hear you again as long as I live," she said. "I have been insulted and—well, you just stroked the fur the wrong way."

"No," the evangelist replied calmly. "I didn't stroke the fur the wrong way. I stroked the fur the right way, but the cat was going in the wrong direction."

The evangelist for a country church high up in the mountains was out visiting prospective members one day. He had spotted a house up in a mountain range that required at least a two-mile walk from the mailbox.

Out of breath from climbing the hill, he arrived at the front porch. He discovered a man rocking back and forth lazily on the porch.

"Howdy, friend, my name is Evangelist Jones. What's yours?"

"Calloway's the name. What can I do for ye?"

The minister continued, "Well, I just came up here to talk to you about some things and ask you a few questions."

"Shoot!" replied the mountaineer.

"Well, the first thing I want to know, Mr. Calloway, is: Have you made peace with God?"

"Peace with God?" questioned Calloway. "Me and God ain't never had no argument!"

"No, no, no, you don't understand, Mr. Calloway. Are you a Christian?"

"Nah, I ain't no Christian, Preacher; I just told you my name is Calloway. The Christians live four mountains up the road."

"Mr. Calloway, I'm having a hard time getting through to you. What I really want to know is this—are you lost?"

"Nah, I ain't lost. I've been living here in these parts all my life. I know these mountains like the back of my hand."

"Mr. Calloway, what I really want to know is: Are you ready for the judgment day?"

"Judgment Day? When's it going to be?"

The young minister replied, "Well, Mr. Calloway, it could be today, or it could be tomorrow."

"Well, land sakes alive, Parson. Don't tell my wife. She'll want to go both days!"

"How did you like the evangelist's sermon?" Mrs. Brown asked her husband on the way home from church.

"Well, frankly," he confessed, "I like our own minister better."

"Why is that?" his wife wanted to know.

"It's the words they use," explained Mr. Brown. "Our preacher says, 'In conclusion,' and then he concludes. The evangelist says, 'Lastly,' and he lasts."

Sleeping at Church

"How late do you usually sleep on Sunday morning?"

"It all depends."

"Depends on what?"

"The length of the sermon."

A minister had worked long and hard on his first sermon, and the delivery of it on Sunday morning had started off well. As he approached the conclusion, however, he became aware that he had lost most of his listeners.

When he finished, he added softly, "I hope it's true."

The congregation was startled by that, and sat up to listen. "I hope it's true," said the preacher again. "Because if it is true that you can learn while you sleep, I will have the best-informed congregation in town."

In the middle of his sermon the preacher noticed a man asleep beside one of his deacons.

"Wake that man up," he called sternly to the deacon.

"Wake him up yourself," the deacon answered. "You put him to sleep."

One father asked his preschool son busy with his blocks, "What are you building, Son?"

"A church," the son replied. "Sh-h-h, we must be very quiet."

The father was encouraged. "Why are we to be quiet in church, Son?"

"Because," said the child, "the people are all asleep."

There was a certain church where the people engaged in what might be called, "responsive praying." Someone in the congregation would spontaneously respond to each request made in a public prayer.

The pastor stood to pray one morning, caught up in the reality of Judgment Day. On the front row, as usual, the church treasurer was sound asleep.

The pastor prayed, "Dear Lord, one of these days we are going to wake up, and it's going to be dark everywhere!"

"Lord, help us!" cried one of the deacons loudly. The church treasurer awoke suddenly.

The pastor continued, "And we are going to pick up the telephone and call Hong

Kong, and they are going to say, 'It's dark over here!'"

"Lord, have mercy!" cried another deacon.

"We're going to pick up the phone and call Honolulu, and they are going to say, 'It's dark over here!'"

"Be near us, Lord!" cried another deacon.

"We're going to pick up the phone and call Paris, and they are going to say, 'It's dark over here!'"

"Lord, deliver us!" cried another deacon.

"Then we're going to pick up the phone and call Moscow, and they are going to say, 'It's dark over here!'"

The church treasurer, silent up until this time, uncontrollably cried, "Lord! Lord! What a phone bill!"

Special Days

On one Christmas, a church bulletin gave exciting ecclesiastical authority to "Sing, choirs of angels, sin in exultation."

What do you get if you cross a centipede with a turkey?

Fewer fights over who gets a drumstick at Thanksgiving.

A well-known minister arrived in town, ready to make a masterful speech at a church observing its anniversary. On Friday a young reporter interviewed him. The minister told the young man many of his finest and most humorous stories.

"But don't print these," he admonished. "I plan to use them in my sermon Sunday."

The reporter agreed and in the Saturday afternoon paper his write-up of the interview concluded: "The minister told a number of good stories which cannot be repeated."

Christmas: season of guided mistletoe.

One outspoken pastor announced from his pulpit one Sunday morning: "Brethren, the janitor and I will hold our weekly prayer meeting next Wednesday night as usual."

Teacher: "Who can tell us something about Good Friday?"
Student: "He was the fellow who helped Robinson Crusoe."

Teacher: "What did the three wise men bring the Christ child?"
Pupil: "Gold, Frankenstein, and mermaids."

Thanksgiving: a holiday instituted by the Pilgrim fathers for the benefit of parents whose sons survived the football season.

Question: What do you get if you cross a turkey with an ostrich?
Answer: A Thanksgiving bird that buries it head in the mashed potatoes.

Girl: "Where did you get that nice Easter tie?"
Boy: "What makes you think it's an Easter tie?"
Girl: "It's got egg on it."

"Did you buy any Christmas seals?"
"No, I wouldn't know how to feed them."

A pastor stood at the church door one Easter Sunday morning, speaking to the people as they left the service. A man came by who hadn't been to church in a long time.

"Good morning, Brother Bud," the minister said. "I do wish we could see you here more regularly."

"What do you mean regularly," the man bristled. "I come every Easter!"

You've probably heard about the preacher who got up on Easter and announced, "Let me wish you a Merry Christmas and a Happy New Year. I look forward to seeing you again next Easter."

There are two Santa Claus's on the street corner. How do you tell which one is a fake?

He's the one with the Easter basket.

Staff

A pastor observed: "We certainly believe in the resurrection at our church. If you doubt it, just visit our offices sometime and watch our staff come back to life at quitting time."

An older minister was counseling a young youth leader. "You will discover," he said, "that in nearly every youth group there is one that is eager to argue. Your first impulse will be to silence him. I advise you to think carefully before doing so. He probably is the only one listening."

A secretary decided to apply for work in a church office. She filled out a job application and later was being interviewed by the pastor.

The pastor noted that she didn't fill in the year of her birth. "I see that your birthday is July 10," said the pastor. "May I ask what year?"

"Every year!" replied the prospective secretary.

Whenever one church's custodian is out to lunch or on some errand, he leaves a big sign on the broom closet: "Janitor is gathering dust."

A discouraged pastor charged that each member of his staff had three speeds:
1. Slow
2. Slower
3. Okay, pallbearers, you can set the body here.

The church janitor called for sweeping reforms.

A friend commented on the church secretary's wig: "It looks very nice on you."

The secretary replied, "Oh, how nice for you to say that—it's my sister's."

The church secretary told her pastor that several wallets had been stolen in the last week, so she was going to keep her purse in the file drawer.

Her pastor observed, "Perfect! Nobody's ever been able to find anything in there!"

Is that pencil pointless?

A pastor is a man who preaches that the best way to rise to the heights is to stay on the level.

Recipe for a Staff Member

Select a young and pleasing personality, trim off all mannerisms of voice, dress, or deportment. Pour over it a mixture of equal parts of the wisdom of Solomon, the courage of young Daniel, the strength of Samson, and the patience of Job.

Season with the salt of experience, the pepper of animation, the oil of sympathy, and a dash of humor.

Stew for about four years in an active church, testing occasionally with the fork of criticism thrust in by a cantankerous church member.

When done to a turn, garnish with a salary increase and serve hot to another church.

Jane: "Our pastor uses a pocket-sized tape recorder."
Jill: "Why?"
Jane: "I don't know except that he must like small talk."

Visitors

A visitor looked into the church auditorium and saw only one empty seat between two nice ladies. He was a very timid man and hesitated to go in.

The usher suggested, "You go in and sit down and just be friendly to the ladies. Ask them if they are married and if they have any children."

He sat down between the two ladies and turned to the one on the right, asking, "Do you have children?" She replied, "Yes." He asked, "Are you married?" She turned away.

Then he turned to the one on the left and asked, "Are you married?" She answered, "No." He asked, "Do you have any children?"

Visitor: Your pastor's messages sure are long-winded.
Member: They may be long . . . but never winded!

A minister of a church gave as his text: "The devil as a roaring lion goeth about seeking those whom he may devour," and then added, "I will be visiting Thursday night. Please come and go with me."

A visitor to a church was touched by an appeal to reduce the mortagage and signed a card that he would give fifty dollars toward it.

On the following Sunday he was shocked to hear the preacher name him as one who promised to give five hundred dollars. He sought out the pastor and made it clear he meant to give much less.

"OK," said the pastor, "I'll tell the congregation you've changed your mind and will not give five hundred dollars."

"Oh, no," replied the man, "I'll give the five hundred dollars to prevent that being said. May I ask you to quote for me my favorite, somewhat-changed Scripture?"

"Certainly," agreed the pastor. "What is it?"

"I was a stranger, and you took me in."

Want to see a religious uprising? Drop a handful of tacks in the family pew.

Weddings

"Do you," the minister asked the perspiring bridegroom, "take this woman to be your wedded wife, for better or worse, for richer, for poorer, in sickness or—"

"Please, sir," interrupted the bride, "you're going to talk him right out of it!"

A young man was really excited at his wedding—he paid the bride for the service and tried to kiss the minister!

An absentminded pastor observed an interesting sight at a rehearsal dinner. The groom rose to speak.

"I have a confession to make to my bride in front of all of you. I confess, dear, that before I married you, I spent many happy hours in the arms of another woman—my mother."

All present enjoyed it, and the minister made a mental note to use it on the occasion of his golden wedding anniversary to be celebrated that week at his church.

The fellowship hall was full of guests to honor the pastor and his wife. He rose to speak. "After fifty years of married life, my dear, I have a confession to make to you in front of all our friends. Before I married you I spent many happy hours in the arms of another woman—and for the life of me, I can't remember who she was."

Old country woman to bride: "Housework's one thing there's no catching up with. You go to bed at night, everything's done. But while you're sleeping, sheets are wrinkling, dust is settling, and stomachs are getting empty."

Wedding anniversary: Easy for a golfer to remember, "How could I forget? It's June 15—on that day in 1953 I missed a two-inch putt on the 15th hole."

"How did the wedding go?" asked the minister's wife.

"Fine, my dear, until I asked the bride if she would obey and she said, 'Do you think I'm crazy?' And the bridegroom, who was in sort of a daze, mumbled, 'I do'—then things began to happen!"

The pastor was telling his wife about the wedding he had performed. "I am afraid that his married life will not be particularly happy."

"Why not, dear?" his wife asked.

"Well, I was watching the bride's family all through the ceremony. They looked far too cheerful to suit me."

"Why do you find life empty?" asked the pastor.

"Because the woman I love has just rejected my proposal of marriage," explained the bachelor.

"Don't let that get you down," said the pastor brightly. "A woman's no often means yes."

"But she didn't say no. She said 'Phooey.'"

An elderly preacher advised his young preacher friend that if he ever forgot the marriage ceremony to start quoting Scriptures until he remembered.

The second wedding, sure enough, the young preacher forgot, and the only Scripture he could remember was, "Father, forgive them, for they know not what they do!"

There was a wedding dinner after the ceremony. When the people finished eating, they called on the bridegroom for a speech. He had never made a speech in his life and didn't know what to say. But now he was scared and thought maybe he had said too much already. The people kept insisting, "Speech, speech."

Finally he realized his friends weren't going to let up. He stood up and stepped behind his bride's chair. Unconsciously he placed a hand on her head.

"I'll tell you right now, folks," he blurted out, "this thing has been forced upon me."

Youth

Pastor: "Our youth group opened a new flea market.

Member: "How did they start?"

Pastor: "They started from scratch."

Awesome Is . . .

Some teenagers use the word "awesome" to describe almost anything that happens. (In bygone years they used "swell" and "great" and "boss," etc.,) Here are some tongue-in-cheek definitions of this word as it might relate to church.

Awesome is: When the pastor enters the auditorium, glances at the small Sunday night crowd, and realizes it is actually Sunday morning!

Awesome is: When a deacon asks his pastor, "Are we still having prayer meeting on Wednesday night?"

Awesome is: Announcing, "We will now sing the last stanza" only to learn that the congregation just finished singing it.

Awesome is: Seeing an usher drop the offering plate after passing it to those in the last row and not reaching down to pick up any money.

Awesome is: Reading in the church bulletin that the title of the Sunday sermon is "Gossip" preceded by the hymn, "I Love to Tell the Story."

Awesome is: Hearing your favorite soprano in the choir miss another high note only to realize that it was not her at all but a truck outside screeching to a halt at a stop sign.

Awesome is: Dreaming that you are preaching a sermon and waking up to find that you really are!

Awesome is: Wondering why some people finish listening to your sermon before you finish preaching it.

Awesome is: When the pastor's wife says, "That sermon you preached today was better than the next one!"

A teenage boy was asked in class which month had twenty-eight days. He answered, "All of them."

Youth Leader: "Our youth group has opened up a store to repair garden tools."
Pastor: "Why?"
Youth Leader: "We want to make mower money!"

A college student fell sound asleep in the middle of his English lit. class. His professor threw a book at him.

"What hit me?" screamed the startled student.

"That," replied the professor, "was a flying Chaucer!"

An exasperated schoolteacher spoke sternly to a "difficult" sixteen-year-old. When she finished, he said to her, "But Teacher, I'm not incorrigible. I'm a Baptist."

Amen (Miscellaneous)

A minister and an unbeliever were engaged in a public debate.

The minister was declared the winner because, at the end of the debate, the unbeliever declared, "Thank God I'm an atheist!"

A small boy came in from play and climbed up into his mother's lap. "Momma," he said seriously, "where was Daddy born?"

"He was born in Oklahoma, honey,"

"Where were you born?"

"I was born in Alabama," his mother smiled fondly.

"Where was I born?"

"You were born right here in Ohio."

He smiled. "Isn't it wonderful that we all got together?"

The traffic accident was an everyday happening. The first car had stopped for a light, and the second plowed into it from behind.

The only odd circumstance was that the first vehicle was being driven by a minister and the second by a priest.

A red-headed Irish policeman came over as the two clergymen began arguing with each other.

"How fast would you say he was going," interjected the policeman, "when he backed into you, Father?"

A Russian archaeological expedition was given a mummy by the Egyptian government. They sent it back to Russia for study. They wanted to determine the mummy's age. The scientists, however, were pushed aside by the secret police who insisted, "Leave it to us; we'll find out."

Presently the secret police announced that the mummy's age was 3,402 years.

"Amazing," cried the Soviet scientists. "How did you determine it?"

"Easy," reported the secret police. "The mummy confessed."

The lady was trying to impress those at the party. "My family's ancestry is very old," she boasted. "It dates back to the days of King James." Then, turning to a lady sitting quietly in a corner, she asked condescendingly, "How old is your family, my dear?"

"Well," came back the woman with a quiet smile, "I can't really say. All our family records were lost in the Flood."

After the service, the rabbi looked blue and despondent. "What was your sermon subject that it took so much energy out of you?" his wife asked.

He replied, "I tried to tell them that it was the duty of the rich to help the poor."

"And did you convince them?" she pursued.

"Only half, I convinced the poor!"

"Is it time to turn the pancakes?" he asked *flippantly.*

Joe: "There's been a book written about watchmaking."
Jack: "Well, it's about time."
AMEN!